Time On Its Own

poems by

Kenneth Frost

MAIN STREET RAG PUBLISHING COMPANY
CHARLOTTE, NORTH CAROLINA

Cover art by Jonathan K. Rice
Author photo: Carolyn Gelland Frost

Acknowledgments: The author wishes to thank the following editors and journals where these poems first appeared:

Bangor Daily News: "Ferry In the Sunset"
The Bitter Oleander: "Closing In," "Two tarantulas"
Cadillac Cicatrix (online journal): "Brass Nipple"
The Café Review: "Wrong Note"
Chase Park: "November"
Confrontation: "Dreamer," "Fat"
Crab Creek Review: "Buddy Rich On the Drums"
Croton Review: "Girl In a Singles' Bar"
Grasslimb: "Mirror"
The Hawaii Review: "Space Trap," "Time On Its Own"
Iodine Poetry Journal: "Spider Web"
Jeopardy: "Foil Reflector"
The Little Magazine: "Until I Think"
Main Street Rag: "Jet Car"
Manhattan Poetry Review: "Bird of Paradise," "Foxhole"
Mudfish: "Ah, Gericault!," "Ferris Wheel"
The Notre Dame Review: "Lute Song," "The voodoo child"
The Phoenix: "Ghost Zoo"
The Prospect Review: "Taxi-Driver"
RiverSedge: "Louis Armstrong," "Moorings," "Ruskin,"
    "Tiger Butterfly," "Whirling Perfume"
Rosebud: "Landlord"
Salmagundi: "Red Beasts," "Frisbee"
Socrates: "Aquinas Wandering," "Metaphysician: Etienne
    Gilson at Verdun"
Wisconsin Review: "Narwhal"

ISBN: 978-1-59948-404-4

Produced in the United States of America

Main Street Rag
PO Box 690100
Charlotte, NC 28227
www.MainStreetRag.com

for Carolyn Gelland Frost
Maude and M. Kenneth Frost
Caroline Gordon Tate

CONTENTS

Ferry In the Sunset 7

Bird of Paradise 8

Moorings 9

Narwhal. 10

Lute Song. 11

Tiger Butterfly. 12

Brass Nipple 13

Louis Armstrong 14

Whirling Perfume. 15

Red Beasts 16

Jet Car. 17

The Figure-Skater. 18

Closing In 20

Aquinas Wandering. 21

Buddy Rich On the Drums 22

The Secret 23

Two Tarantulas 24

Ruskin 25

Ghost Zoo 26

Girl In a Singles' Bar 27

Ferris Wheel 28

Taxi-Driver 29

Frisbee 30

Fat. 31

Dreamer. 32

Time On Its Own 33

Landlord 34

The Voodoo Child 35

Hush Hush 36

Explorer. 37

He Floats Out 38
November 39
Metaphysician—Etienne Gilson at Verdun 40
Foxhole 41
Foil Reflector. 42
Spider Web 43
Space Trap. 44
Mirror 45
Wrong Note. 46
Until I Think 47
Ah, Gericault! 48
Sighting 49
Suddenly 50

FERRY IN THE SUNSET

The oval ferry
stretches its mouth
and spins
around and around
the sunset,
chasing its dog's
fleas of music,
slapping the water
in applause.
The cars blister
their windshields
in the red sun
and the bay foams,
flashing
porpoises
in the ferry's wake.

BIRD OF PARADISE

My thoughts crawl around
the surface of my brain

as though it were some tropic fruit,
a bird of paradise of fruits.

Oh, how beautiful,
those high-key colored continents.

This ought to prove
something exists—

consciousness as $X + 1$,
and X as π climbing

its numbers through the world
to where it can be whole

and looking back at π,
an ancient gate.

MOORINGS

I fall
asleep
by the
cathedral's
paws,
dream
lion
skins
singing
the furnace
to rest.

NARWHAL

A new Ptolemaic system
whispered
into me
is stored in scrolls
of chemicals
in the fat tissues of my brain.

An Eskimo would understand.
He flails
his paddle wings
to chase the narwhal's trumpet
through a Jericho
of cracks.

The narwhal's forehead flesh
remembers
the first
sun.

LUTE SONG

What boulder leaks
a morning thawed

to a lute song
riding its champagne
memory

Aether pings
its rosary
one by one by one

till chords run
wild

All doors
break open

manes comb the air
and harvest it

See see
the shining

TIGER BUTTERFLY

After two years,
the tiger butterfly
swam out of the clear
cellophane bag
that preserved him
and took a deep breath.
He knew he had been asleep
and his golden wings,
with their cave-painted
black fingers
trying to drag him
back to earth,
were stronger,
lighter;
he could leap and glide—
a second moon
of tiger wings.
Children saw him in their sleep
and heard his words
luminous in another
language
they didn't know
when awake,
memory's tongue
translating to a calm
urgent light,
a crystal map,
and there, there…

BRASS NIPPLE

The baby was born
with a toy trumpet
for a mouth.

We fed him
milk through the brass
nipple till he
burped on his own.

He cried. Crying
mastered
the horn,

summoned
all the people
to the swaying
hills.

LOUIS ARMSTRONG

His breath stretches
in its wind tunnel's
cornucopia
till notes grow bold
enough to hear
their birthday openings.

How beautiful
the red-gold hair
Helen shakes
in the high notes
to wake perfume's
transparent garden
into doorways'
magnetic light.

WHIRLING PERFUME

The smoke curled
and braided itself,
tongue-tied except
in lilac fragrance
blanketing the air,
almost choking it
in revelation's
whirling perfume,
heart's wolves
circling—no, not
amber-eyed
animals, sight
clear as crystal balls
where you could read
Saint Francis
in their trance,
but high-pitched,
prophetic laughter.

RED BEASTS

Do the red beasts
graze on the stars
on the rock dome of sky?
I almost hear
their outlines, all
of them, singing
what is beyond
the rock of rocks.
Sitting beside
the fire, my friend and theirs,
their whip and choir,
I cook and eat their steak;
the blood of time
runs from my teeth.
Ten thousand years,
twenty thousand,
what did I count,
stick hunter,
a mess of stars,
scrut, scrut, scrut
that I red-chalked
scrut, scrut, scrut.
If I have died
I know the mind
a living sleep.

JET CAR

A lion's roar
streams off the flanks
as my jet car
leaps for its prey,
polishes light
on the windshield
to drop
time from its lariat.
Roll, doggie, roll,
on the dead fish
of the earth,
break the divine
to Cristoforo
staggering
on the sun drunk
under his feet.

THE FIGURE-SKATER

Like the headlight
on a freight train
stirring its witches'
broth of wheels
down double-barreled rails,
faster, faster,
looming on,
homing on
the heroine,
bound in her strait-
jacket of ropes,
the figure-skater,
wound in her
star-spangled spin
flashing a spool
of zodiacs,
dances how many angels
on the steel-tipped
infinity
of her skate-blades
while her esprit woos
the fortune
a dust bowl
remembers
in whirlwinds
till a star leaps

out of the coils
of gravity.
Escapading on
the mirror's altar,
she swings
into exploding mercury
that bends and scatters
apparitions
just holding on
to godspeed
with the rich glaze of her smile.

CLOSING IN

Firelight dances
a gold halo
wide with wolves'
eyes, wolves' eyes
mesmerizing
tunnels
drawing
mirrors from dreams.

As fire strikes
its drumsticks,
wolves' eyes draw
their prayerbeads
through whispers
their memories
corner.

AQUINAS WANDERING

What vagabond
can find a home
where the moon echoes
a carnival
of new-mown razorblades
and what Gregorian
do hornets sizzle
swooping and swooping
haloes over
their caved-in
nests like catacombs
and who loses
when owls hoo-hoo
the slight rustling
forests of feathers
their togas wear.

BUDDY RICH ON THE DRUMS

Back to the wall
where the heart leans,
taking dictation
from thunderstorms
that crumble static
in a god's throat,

I thresh my hides
till temple echoes
chase themselves
in nerve-bellies
flushing all
that a snake knows,

whipping his head
so fast his tongue
stutters his own
drumsticks to point
backward and gulp
the lost divine.

THE SECRET

Who kept the secret?
The birds who left
eyes scattered
in the fir trees,
each one alone,
alone, alone.

What traveler
squeezed through the hatch
of a lone eye
and felt shadows
juggle and stretch
cryptic wounds?

Look, look, all eyes
trading their thrones,
leaving some notes
in the trees' throats.
Where is the throat
in Cyclops' eye?

Drunk on pain,
the sun staggers
out of morning,
crisscrossing voices,
"Sun, oh sun,
oh sun, oh sun, oh sun."

TWO TARANTULAS

pronouncing
their whirring
legs, advance
across the field,
whispering together,
the wind in their hair,
the ancient wind.

RUSKIN

My hair turns white.
Two traps stare out
of this weeping willow
rooted in my brain.

My childhood's gutted
rabbit gasps
before a mirror
with its inside
tears, landscapes
weeping with women,

and the hammering,
hammering with
bent nails like fish-hook
rain.

GHOST ZOO

Zookeepers know
people will stop to stare
at locked empty cages
as easily as
full ones.

My body is my dream space.
It pulls me
around ghost zoo
reading the stones.

I have no
time for Pentecost.
Blow the brushfire voices
of its Afro out.
Lost time.
Lost time.

The blackmail of
my childhood is my middle age.
Someone must help me
pay for it.

GIRL IN A SINGLES' BAR

The guitarist
plays the silk scarves
of my striptease
out of my scotch
till I look up
the cataract
lens of my drink
and see the night.
When I look harder,
jet after jet
sickles
the rotten wheat
starlight,
circling
as it comes in
or takes off
for anywhere.
Fly me, my head
begs from the ad
on every bus
at a red light
and floats away,
rippling light,
up Madison.
I put my glass
against the wall
to bug this ark.
"What have we done,
what have we done
to one another?"

FERRIS WHEEL

It's difficult, seeing
someone hitchhike against a wall
of high headlights, to say
"That's me" anchored
to a shadow's metronome.

What makes someone someone?
The Collyers kept
dwelling in narrowing
years of *Times*
until they had one tunnel of faith

to a throne room
where blindness would awake,
read each day fully back
to hypostatic day.

Listen to the garbage truck,
a ferris wheel
crushing disappointment
into its own sound somewhere
in the darkness of itself.

TAXI-DRIVER

My taxi shakes
its witch-doctor's
rattle
at the ghost caged in the back seat,

dodges
between headlights,
a gangwar
of full moons,

leaves behind
a traffic jam
of empty fingerprints.

FRISBEE

The frisbee of my clavicle
has something to it.

They can't throw it away.
It keeps coming back for my head.

It likes to play ball with my head.
You'd think stale air was Fido

or these creeps William Tell.
They're not.

I'm not his son.
Jesus, I'm confused,

but I don't want to be seen
with a bone through my head.

I would have thought I had
more important business

than to hang
around this antique factory

worrying what morticians do
to fakes, but here I am,

wondering
have they replaced my brain

with a sponge soaked in vinegar.
It thinks the same.

FAT

I pull the mattress off my bed
each morning and stamp hard, harder,
upon the blubber I have cut—
escape hatch in the whale of dreams.
This trampoline whoops me up
and my flesh parachutes me down
so I am a merry-go-round
stood on one end. Coney Island
bought me after the first World's Fair,
programmed me into birth.

Often on Hudson Street I see
bums grilling pigeons on the tops
of the trash baskets.
                    They eat them,
feathers and all trembling in
cupped hands. I carefully unhook
the porcupine quills of my heart
out of my mouth and weigh myself.

DREAMER

A turkey vulture,
flashing his black
rainbow feathers,
sitting at
my breakfast
table
banging
his knife and
fork on the table
with mummy
hands,
has a napkin
tucked around
his neck,
having already
eaten
a hearty
meal of
my dreams.

TIME ON ITS OWN

Did you ever drift
like smoke
from the will's
cremation in a cigarette?
If I were anywhere

to be found
I would think
something through
the universe
grinning like skidmarks from a tire.

Somewhere beyond
my centipede of echoes
someone insists, "Climb higher, a circus dive
will pull along
cold feet."

Time is on its own,
it comes on
swaying,
slowly pawing the ground,
searching the world like trash.

LANDLORD

of all
the vacant
lots,
I sit
in the skull
of a stripped car,
steering
it through
whispers
and broken fans
of headlights.

THE VOODOO CHILD

shrinks building blocks
to fit his hand
and deals out his dream.

The blocks rise
higher and higher
till the sky scrapes
and rumbles into place.

He claps his hands.
He climbs up, up.
At the top,
he takes his head off.
He telephones.

HUSH HUSH

Lights dim
in abandoned
Alcatraz
drained by the empty
chair
where the king sits
with steel bracelets
and a steel crown
smoking away.

EXPLORER

A giant luna moth
pinned the boy's arms down,
stared into his eyes.
Wide eyes,
wider moons,
carried a message
from a new
found land
bundled in ether.
The boy slid
through the black
fragrance of the brain
deeper
deeper
into its winged
empty space.

When the silence
knew it
was a silence
it ripened
and burst
open
forming a bridge
and talking
to the past
long before
he was born.

HE FLOATS OUT

in the hollow
notes of the wind
instrument
till the rooms
around him
wander
and a strange tree
of dreams
takes root
on every
windowsill.

NOVEMBER

These November branches
drip crows upside down.
The rain fills
mirrors with bats,

bony monkeys
preaching fingernails
to the long tunnel
of a hare's scream.

METAPHYSICIAN—
ETIENNE GILSON AT VERDUN

The psyche leaks sideward
as a footsoldier kneels
to his muddy amputation
in a rat's potion of rain
deep enough to assist
a skeleton to shake
his fever off
into the endless eye
a patient acrobat
left behind to play
fool to nimble memory.

O spider, play your harp
in the wind's telescope.

FOXHOLE

Two cars doodle toward one
another, waltzing alone on ice.
Foxhole to foxhole, we meet
in no-man's land,
squeezed in a press.
My face facing my face
floats around
a falling hole.

How far away it seems.

A silk tabernacle
floats
on the strange mournful muttering
of the battlefield
and settles
down
to someone
rotted
down to one ear more
than chaos.
His sockets hold the landscape
his mirage.

FOIL REFLECTOR

He serves his head up to the sun
on a foil tray.
All of his mind that can't
displace
the gonging
runs from his neck in river lights.

His white and witching face
smiles with the secrets
he forgets
as he breathes up free-basing scars
only his blind eyelids can spell.
He drifts upward,

supple, streamlined, senile
out of perpetual
sunbursts.

See
the graveclothes ripped
to dragonrags descending from
creation's
aftermath,
sand with a nervous tic.

SPIDER WEB

Today
when the spider
web stretches
out of sight,
I sit
in my apartment
watching
the ambulances
fly by
like hummingbirds
and disappear
into the stone
flower of
the hospital.

SPACE TRAP

Something is stolen or disappears
from this room every day,
at least one thing—

a side table, a paper, a glass
have no way out
but the one window.

I watch a table
or a glass of water
stand on the wall,

nothing falls, nothing gets there
by itself or someone else.
The room rounds its corners.

I am inside a globe
for days
and then four walls again.

MIRROR

His face stayed
flush in the mirror
when he glanced back—
he knew it would.

Many times
when he woke up,
he felt its magnet
drawing his skin and nerves.

He crept
out in the dark.
The mirror's eyes
stared back at him.

The eyes blinked
and closed the mirror.
Somewhere
he heard a door
slam.

At long last
the mirror cleared
its throat
and began.

WRONG NOTE

A forty-mile-an-hour wind
on ships' rigging plays
middle-C on the piano.

I hear notes of high pitch
on telegraph wires,
higher in corn,
higher yet in grass.

My telephone wire sings
its loudest on
frosty mornings,
inhabiting the frequency
of a whirlwind.

The wrong note.
No one played it.
It comes out
softly but unmistakably
with another note.

UNTIL I THINK

The bidding on the stock exchange
sounds like Gregorian
over the radio,
so does Grand Central, late.

No need to count
how many scuttle,
weave and advance
across the almost open plain

like prizefighters boxing a dream
they have of mine
as I sit on the head of things
not things until I think.

My shadow almost floats
into my hand
wanting to
point something out.

AH, GERICAULT!

Am I the only one who sees
this forearm stretching
out of the open circle of the sea—
this gray hand trying
to get a grip
upon the substance of the sky?

I say, Ah, Gericault,
as one chews gum
so memory can salivate
and tour the echoes in my head
that someone lives behind.

The hand or head is staring,
stock-still,
out of its game preserve.
I think it thinks it feels
the rope inside the air
tickle its fingertips.

SIGHTING

Buried latitudes
dream in crystals
till even memories
depend on wind.

Their city whips
heat dizzy,
stretching dry grounds
to coil and flay

knights to transparent
trenches banners snap
from their more than
ancient blue trove.

Towers and terraces
creak gold,
ferrying
lost to found.

SUDDENLY,

there you are
in the
electric
eternity
of a dream.

Who shall I
tell them
you are
with your
long hair,
embodied
light?